Upstairs
❖ AND ❖
Downstairs

Edward Hayward

The old world of above and below stairs has almost disappeared, but during the reigns of Queen Victoria (1837–1901) and her son King Edward VII (1901–10), the period covered by this book, almost everyone either had servants or had been one at some time in their life. In 1891 the Census tells us there were almost two million indoor servants alone, including over 100,000 children under the age of fifteen. By their employers, servants were sometimes thought of as 'a problem', but they were usually treated as part of the family community and even became objects of affection.

It is important not to judge the past by our own standards: most 'recruits' came from backgrounds where life was hard and sometimes cruel. Once they became servants, boredom and lack of freedom were likely to be worse enemies than cold, hunger and hard work.

Living conditions were not necessarily so much better for the well born members of a landowning family, particularly after the agricultural slump of the 1860s. Some lived in reduced circumstances, and the habit of self-denial was strong, though all tried to keep up appearances. However, there was for many the compensation of being born at the top of the tree, and receiving the deference most felt they deserved.

ABOVE:
In an age before alarm clocks, tea in bed was a useful means of starting the day and tackling some task before prayers and breakfast.

There were no automatic timers, little cold water plumbing and few hot water systems. Safety and economy meant that few fires were kept alight overnight. In the largest houses there were nightmen, who cleaned the boots, trimmed the wicks of candles and oil lamps, brought in wood and coal and, just before dawn, lit the kitchen and scullery stoves and heated the water.

EARLY RISERS

The early risers, perhaps the scullery maid and the page, were stirring by 5.30 am, scrubbing and sweeping the kitchen areas, distributing hot water for tea and shaving to the senior servants, and laying breakfast in the servants' hall. Then by 7.00 am the maids and footmen busied themselves with water and tea-trays for the family, and the nursery breakfast. On the way back they brought down the chamber-pots for emptying and replaced them for the first of several times in the day. The butler unlocked the shutters and doors, and pulled back blinds so that the housemaids could clear, re-lay and light fires, black the grates and then polish and dust downstairs.

BELOW RIGHT:
A generous breakfast is enjoyed by guests at a country house before a day out hunting.

❖ MORNING PRAYERS ❖

The gentry, almost always Anglicans, made a point of practising their religion openly as an example, and some of the big country houses had their own chapels. Prayers were held at 8.30 am, after the servants' breakfast but before that of the family. Most of the household attended, reluctantly or not, at least to pay lip service together to beliefs about duty, hard work and a God-given hierarchy which no-one must question.

Usually the working day for senior servants and members of the family started before prayers. The butler might have taken advantage of the stillness and quiet to decant some wine. The cook might already have taken some deliveries and consulted with the gardener about what available fruit and vegetables she could include in the lunch and dinner menus. The baker or still-room maid would have baked the proved dough for breakfast rolls while the postboy might have accepted a mug of tea or beer after bringing the telegrams up from the post office. In the coach house the coach staff and grooms might be preparing a coach and horses (suitably grand) to take the master to a sitting of the justices later in the day, while the master himself might have already spent an hour on the accounts in the office with the estate manager. His wife, meanwhile, might have discussed with her maid alterations to a dress which needed to be completed that day.

LEFT:
The tweenies (between-stairs maids) helped with the cold ashes, bringing in fresh coal and whitening the front steps.

❖ SERVICE BELLS ❖

A system of bells or flags in the servants' hall showed when and where service was needed, and some elaborate codes were developed to suit the individual needs of the house. Later came the speaking tube and then the telephone. The original system was invented in about 1780 and meant that servants no longer had to loiter in corridors within earshot of the family. Henceforth rules were laid down about not straying into the family's areas, inside or outside the house, except on business. If seen, servants were told to stand still and look at the floor, or even turn to the wall, and they had to stay away from windows in order not to be seen from the outside.

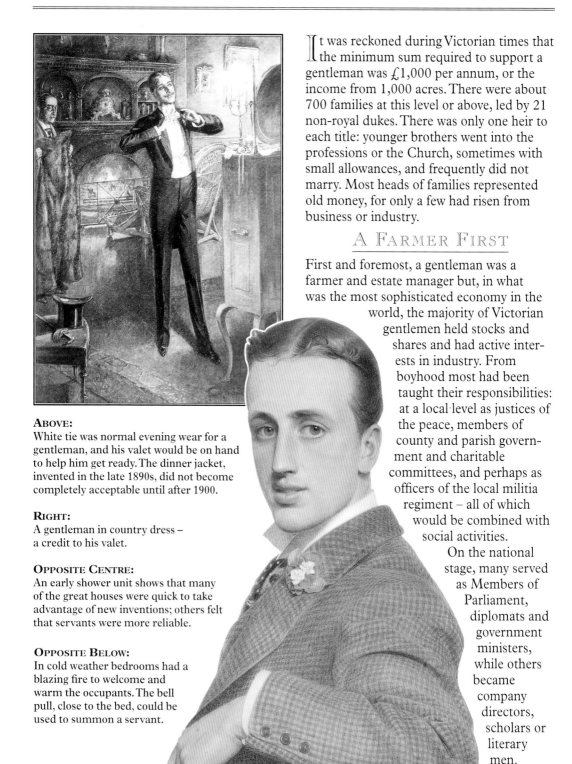

It was reckoned during Victorian times that the minimum sum required to support a gentleman was £1,000 per annum, or the income from 1,000 acres. There were about 700 families at this level or above, led by 21 non-royal dukes. There was only one heir to each title: younger brothers went into the professions or the Church, sometimes with small allowances, and frequently did not marry. Most heads of families represented old money, for only a few had risen from business or industry.

A FARMER FIRST

First and foremost, a gentleman was a farmer and estate manager but, in what was the most sophisticated economy in the world, the majority of Victorian gentlemen held stocks and shares and had active interests in industry. From boyhood most had been taught their responsibilities: at a local level as justices of the peace, members of county and parish government and charitable committees, and perhaps as officers of the local militia regiment – all of which would be combined with social activities.

On the national stage, many served as Members of Parliament, diplomats and government ministers, while others became company directors, scholars or literary men.

ABOVE:
White tie was normal evening wear for a gentleman, and his valet would be on hand to help him get ready. The dinner jacket, invented in the late 1890s, did not become completely acceptable until after 1900.

RIGHT:
A gentleman in country dress – a credit to his valet.

OPPOSITE CENTRE:
An early shower unit shows that many of the great houses were quick to take advantage of new inventions; others felt that servants were more reliable.

OPPOSITE BELOW:
In cold weather bedrooms had a blazing fire to welcome and warm the occupants. The bell pull, close to the bed, could be used to summon a servant.

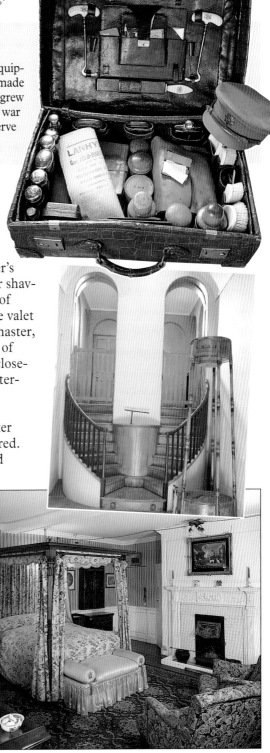

❖ THE TOILET SET ❖

A toilet set was an essential part of a gentleman's equipment, and could well have contained shaving soap made to his valet's own secret recipe. Relationships often grew strong between a master and his valet, and during war service many valets went with their gentlemen to serve as batmen.

THE VALET

The valet, the master's personal servant, had much prestige within the household. First, he had to have, clean and repaired, the correct outfit for every occasion, to attend to his master's toilette (perhaps using his own secret recipe for shaving soap or boot polish), including the ironing of shoelaces and the washing of small change. The valet travelled everywhere of consequence with his master, deciphering train timetables and taking charge of valuables and cash, and he was privy to many close-kept secrets. Abroad he acted as courier and interpreter, and might well have more contacts and knowledge of foreign ways than his master. He needed to be fit, for he rose before his master and could not sleep until long after he had retired. Away from home he waited on him at table and loaded his shotguns.

Naturally, a good valet's experience and panache had to be recognized with excellent wages and a high level of trust. Tips and presents were lavished on him along with the gift of the master's cast-off clothes, to be worn or sold. Many made enough to set up as shopkeepers or hoteliers: Byron's man Brown, for instance, founded the famous Mayfair hotel bearing his name. If the valet stayed with his master, he might expect promotion to butler or steward, but in many ways his life was more interesting as it was.

The role of the master's wife was primarily to be decorative; she was intended to be a good hostess after the model of such stars as Daisy, Countess of Warwick, Lady Londonderry (on a state visit the Shah of Persia offered to buy her!) or Louise van Alten, who married in succession the Dukes of Manchester and Devonshire. She might bring money to her husband (a dowry of £10,000 and £300 per annum was considered correct) and she needed to be able to manage her homes and set a public example as, for instance, committee member and charity visitor. She was also expected to be a good and loving mother.

ABOVE:
The mistress of the house had to be manager as well as hostess, mother, and leader of local society. Menus and household arrangements needed frequent discussion with the housekeeper.

SPECIAL TALENTS

The lady's maid had the task of ensuring that her mistress's appearance was always appropriate and immaculate; that, in time, grey hairs, wrinkles and a spreading figure were kept at bay and that minor ailments did not come in the way of a sparkling public persona. The maid supervised the elegance of the boudoir and was often the only other person allowed free access. Women totally depended on their maids: for instance, many garments could only be fastened at the back. Like the valet, a lady's maid travelled with her mistress and was honoured accordingly by other servants, at home and away; she worked for no-one else. She was usually in her 20s but, for all her youth, her special talents kept her apart from the other maids and she was treated as a senior.

French ladies' maids were considered the most knowledgeable in matters of fashion, but it was well known that they could be temperamental, and there could be difficulties in times of war with France. A French-Swiss maid might be a little less chic, but she was often more reliable.

By her 30s a lady's maid began looking for a husband or a position as a housekeeper: she was losing her stamina, and her earning power as a maid decreased accordingly. On the other hand, if nothing else came along, she could well have saved enough to open a haberdasher's or milliner's shop in a fashionable part of the West End of London.

LEFT:
The Morning Room was always kept neat and tidy for visitors, who might be given a glass of madeira and a small piece of cake. They were looked after by the senior servants if the master and mistress were out.

BELOW:
The boudoir was usually linked by an inner door to the bedroom and was intended to be secluded, even from the master. The lady's maid was often the only other person allowed free access to this room. She was treated as a senior servant and as such had access to the housekeeper's room.

LEFT:
The great hostesses of the late 19th century were sparkling and decorative. Helped by their servants, they made sure their guests had every comfort.

The fire and its rail were used to dry clothes, cook snacks and to sit around, talking and reading stories. Books, clothes, toys and furniture were all laboriously patched up and passed down.

In a large nursery, Nanny looked after the eldest son, and the girls and younger boys had the more junior nursemaids in descending order of precedence. Lessons were basic and followed a rather monotonous routine. Food was plain but wholesome, and walks were designed for letting off steam (especially out of sight of strangers); sometimes a young footman was detailed as escort and playmate. At bedtime the parental visit was often much warmer and more intimate than is supposed today.

NANNY

Nannies were usually revered and often loved, and sometimes served a family for two or three generations. They could be strict, but were frequently a source of old wisdom and old remedies. Often the younger nursery maids were more sympathetic, and traditionally children turned to other servants for knowledge of the world. Butlers might arrange first bets for the adolescent boys and maids sometimes provided the first experience of sex.

THE GOVERNESS

Most Victorian boys were taught along with their sisters by the nursery staff until the age of eleven or twelve, when they went off to boarding school, and a governess arrived for the girls. She was perhaps the junior daughter of a gentle family, with above average education, or a distant relative, who provided teaching and companionship to adolescent girls sometimes only a few years younger than herself. While many young women stayed at home until marriage, the position of governess was that of a respected and well paid senior servant. Once girls' schools and higher education for women became widely accepted the position began to die out.

Tutors were much more common in the 18th century, when the public school system was less well established. By the 19th century only very wealthy and well-connected boys had a tutor.

ABOVE:
Proud of her neat black dress, lace apron and cap, this young maid's name would probably have been one used in the house by tradition, and not her own.

BELOW:
There were quiet moments during the day when there was time to welcome a friend for a cup of tea and some cake.

The kitchen and the surrounding rooms, including the servants' hall and the butler's pantry, made up the main working areas below stairs. At mealtimes in the servants' hall, the hierarchy of the family dining table was copied: cook and housekeeper sat at one end, butler or steward at the other, and the juniors between. At the end of a meal, the table was cleared for reading or hobbies.

THEIR PRIDE AND JOY

Work was hardest in the morning. Maids, wearing print dresses, cleaned the public areas, while footmen, if not too grand, might be persuaded to help with the lifting. At the end of the morning lunch was laid and served, for which the maids might change into black dresses, with lace caps and aprons. These were their pride and joy: they were homemade and hours were spent on starching and caring for them.

RATES OF PAY PER ANNUM
(Board included)
circa 1870

Butler	£70
Housekeeper	£40-£60
Gardener	£90
Governess	£80-£100
Nanny	£35
Lady's Maid and Valet	£50-£60
Housemaid	£20
Footman	£20-£30
Groom	£20
Scullerymaid and Tweeny	£8-£12

'Tigers'

In the afternoon the male servants came into their own, attending the mistress on her calls or leaving visiting cards, or on shopping expeditions, or charitable visits. On these trips a footman or groom (called a 'tiger' because of his traditional yellow and black striped livery), opened the doors of the mistress's carriage, protected her from the mud and from beggars and carried her parcels. If needed, another footman went with the master, while the remainder opened the door to callers or went on errands. Spare footmen were allotted to the nursery. In the evening it was the footmen's turn to wait at table, and make a special show for dinner guests.

ABOVE:
The laundry was often in a separate building to keep the steam away from the house. All linen was monogrammed and kept in a linen room.

❖ The Maid's Day ❖

5.30 am	Clean kitchen floors
6.00 am	Heat water
6.30 am	Wake seniors, lay and light fires, lay servants' breakfast, deliver nursery breakfast
7.30 am	Water and tea-trays to family, empty chamber-pots
7.45 am	Servants' breakfast
8.30 am	Prayers
9.00 am	Family breakfast
9.30 pm	Clear and clean
12.00 pm	Lunch, servants' hall and nursery
1.00 pm	Family lunch
2.30 pm	Clear lunch, rest
4.30 pm	Tea-trays for household
5.30 pm	Servants' tea, nursery tea
6.00 pm	Lay dinner, help in kitchen
7.00 pm	Family dinner, serve and clear
9.00 pm	Servants' supper
10.00 pm	Bed

ABOVE:
An early freezer. There were many ways of keeping food fresh and a surprising number of houses had their own supply of ice all year or, from the 1880s, it could be delivered from a factory. In wintertime collecting ice was a job for the footmen.

Until perhaps 250 years ago most things consumed and used on a great country estate would have been grown or made there. In Victorian and Edwardian times the bulk of foodstuffs would still have been home grown, and these, along with anything bought in, would have passed through the hands of the cook (who often acted as housekeeper too). The kitchen was the hub of all downstairs activity, a place of heat and bustle where several different menus and mealtimes were accommodated. Large houses might have a French chef and perhaps an Italian confectioner, but most made do with a cook. Special dishes for grand occasions could be left to extra talent hired for the evening.

KEEPING FOOD FRESH

The lack of refrigeration created particular problems, especially at times of glut, and most kitchen areas were arranged so that cool storage rooms – for meat, game, fish, cheese, fruit and vegetables, dry goods and so on – were kept well away from the heat of the kitchen fires. The furthest away was the dairy, often fitted in Delft tiles or marble, where cheese, butter and cream were made fresh every few days.

BELOW:
The kitchen and staff of a large household. A number of different menus were provided, with early mealtimes for the servants' hall and nursery, and lighter food on trays for the sick or infirm.

Careful ordering of provisions was a skill cooks needed since everything had to be cooked and eaten quickly. The servants always had a specially prepared lunch, but in the evening they were asked to finish the left-overs from the family's dinner; these could be the finest foods, with wines to match. Usually rations were laid down, and if the cook did not cheat, they were generous, perhaps 1½lbs of meat daily and 1lb of tea and 4lbs of sugar monthly, 3 pints of beer a day for men and 1½ pints for women. If the family was away, an allowance (or board wage) was provided instead, perhaps up to a more-than-adequate 10–15 shillings per person each week.

ABOVE LEFT:
A state-of-the-art kitchen towards the end of the 19th century. The kitchen was usually situated in the basement or at the back of the house.

BELOW:
Stoves had to be scoured and black leaded, and needed a constant supply of fuel.

If the house was old-fashioned there might be a still-room where the maid prepared light sweets and ices, fruit wines and cordials along with the simple medical aids originally distilled from herbs and spices. The scullery was often awash with water – the scullery maid did the washing up and prepared the vegetables there. Here, too, was the butler's pantry, an office with racks for glasses, access to the cellar, a large safe for the silver, and some-times a bed so that he could guard the valuables even at night. Occasionally footmen slept on camp beds in the kitchen area to keep them away from the maids in the attics.

RIGHT:
The butler made sure that wine was in good condition, and knew the ways to restore it (cinnamon was a traditional additive). This involved tasting, and perhaps the temptation to over-indulge.

BELOW:
The dining room was often regarded as male territory and after dinner the ladies withdrew to allow the men time for port, cigars and talk.

Dinner, the main meal of the day, often took place as early as 6.30 or 7.00 pm. It was customary to dress for dinner – full length evening dress for the ladies, and white tie for the gentlemen (dinner jackets not being completely accepted until after 1900) – and to give time for preparation a signal was given an hour ahead. Usually this was a gong or bell, but in a few households it was a drum or even trumpets. No matter how small the number of diners, dinner was a formal

meal. Grace was said and the family silver used. At weekend parties in the grander houses, exotic flowers were given to each lady guest to wear.

The usual sources for menus were *Mrs Beeton's Household Management* (1861) or Francatelli's *Cook's Guide* (1862).

The meal was always five or six courses but could be extended to nine or ten. The master or his butler carved the meat, and vegetables were handed separately to each diner. Footmen waited at table, but any available servant could be roped in, including coachmen, who were allowed to 'rest' beforehand so stable smells could fade! Resident male guests would be served by their own valets.

BRANDY AND CIGARS

After dinner, the ladies withdrew for tea or coffee and liqueurs, leaving the men alone to enjoy fruit, nuts, port, brandy and cigars. The decanters were passed from diner to diner towards the left.

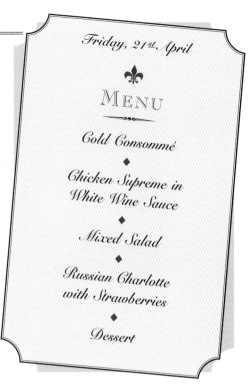

Friday, 21st April

MENU

Cold Consommé

◆

Chicken Supreme in White Wine Sauce

◆

Mixed Salad

◆

Russian Charlotte with Strawberries

◆

Dessert

BELOW:
For big dinner parties, all servants were expected to help, and carry on until order had been restored, no matter how long it took. In most houses there were compensating times of slackness while the family was away, and perhaps an extra gift to say 'thank you'.

BELOW CENTRE:
A group of servants
of various ages and
types includes young
maids and a smiling
butler. The young
woman dressed in
plain clothes is likely
to be a governess or
perhaps a lady's maid.

BELOW:
All servants started on
the bottom rung of the
ladder. Junior foot-
men, or pages, began
very young, answering
doors, running
messages and perhaps
carrying coal or clean-
ing boots. Older foot-
men needed an
imposing appearance
to impress visitors and
promote their master's
image. They were paid
according to their
appearance, and
height was particularly
important. Where knee
breeches were worn,
thin calves would be
padded.

No matter how long the hours, how cold the floors
and how hard the beds, most young recruits to
the big house had made a great step up in the world.
They were often orphans or paupers or children from
the local village, and well used to hunger, cold, harsh
treatment and cramped conditions. Many would
never have seen gas lighting before, and very few
would have used a water closet. To begin life in
service, they needed money to buy clothes – two
dresses with caps, cuffs and aprons for the girls, and
shoes, shirts and stiff collars for the boys. Often the
vicar paid for these, though sometimes the young
people earned the money in a factory, which could
take two years of hard saving. Most started at the
bottom aged between ten and twelve years, as scullery
or between-stairs maids or bootboys, and earned
perhaps £5–£10 per year, much of which was sent
home or spent on necessaries.

SUPERIOR EDUCATION.

Page Boy (to Jeames). "WHERE SHALL I PUT THIS 'ERE DISH OF AMMONDS?"
Jeames (with dignity). "I'M SURPRISED, HARTHUR, THAT AT YOUR HAGE YOU
'AVEN'T LEARNT 'OW TO PERNOUNCE THE *HAR* IN HARMONDS!"

❖ THE HOUSEKEEPER'S ROOM ❖

The housekeeper's sitting-room was a key place in the running of a big house. Here, often the family's precious china was washed and stored and all tea was brewed (it may be that 'afternoon tea' originated in the 1850s from the ladies popping in at 5.00 pm before dressing for dinner). In the evenings, at the end of the meal in the servants' hall, seniors processed with glasses and linen, to finish eating in the housekeeper's sitting-room and to enjoy the best wines, tea and coffee.

BELOW RIGHT:
A butler's pantry. In many households a butler was a Chief of Staff. He might be called on to deputize for the valet or even be made responsible for the efficient butchery of animals, if the other seniors were women.

Housemaids and footmen had more to eat, a better choice of beds and bedrooms, a greater chance of tips, and perhaps two to three times the pay. Footmen were employed partly for show, and were paid according to height and looks. They often worked in 'matched pairs' and were provided with several sets of gorgeous livery. They had to powder their hair, which left it damp and cold and liable to fall out early, but they were out and about all the time, with opportunities to enjoy the admiration of the girls, and it was probably not too hard to answer to 'John' or 'Thomas', whatever their real names, or, occasionally, to be mocked by street urchins. Maids also had to adopt new names, but their uniforms were attractive and they too might have chances of fleeting liaisons (perhaps while going to post a letter!).

RIGHT:
The still-room was traditionally run by the housekeeper. The name originated from a distilling apparatus for making special concoctions from fruits, herbs, spices and sugar, which were used for cleaning, flavouring, colouring, and curing small ailments.

BELOW:
Senior servants were often nicknamed 'pugs' because they learned to have a sober cast of face, with turned-down mouth, like a pug dog.

If a servant showed aptitude and willingness, he or she would be promoted, and become a 'pug' or senior. Age and grave demeanour were important, but pugs were also recognizable by their lack of a uniform and were addressed by their own surname, with or without a 'Mr' or 'Mrs' (only the governess and lady's maid were called 'Miss').

There were four grades of pug serving indoors (the head coachman and gardener were also seniors, but were only included on special occasions). The senior men were the steward, groom of chambers, butler and valet, though many houses made do with only one or two of these. They ran the 'front of house' and the cellar, cared for the glass and silver, and occasionally brewed the beer. Part of their job was to look after visitors in the absence of the master and mistress.

❖ PREPARING THE NEWSPAPER ❖

A special task involved preparing the daily newspaper, which arrived wet from the printing press, in one large sheet. Individual pages had to be cut and then folded, and ironed to remove the damp. A really professional steward or butler would then stitch them together.

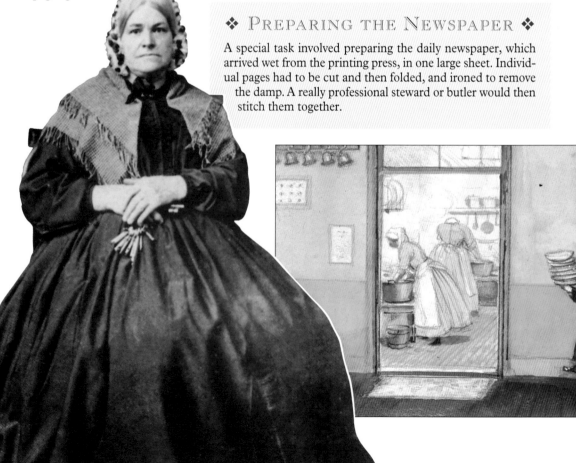

Cook, housekeeper and lady's maid were the senior women, along with the governess. Housekeepers, often by force of personality, controlled the entire servant body. They dealt with cleaning, heating and lighting and the ordering and supply of all materials, often including food. No doubt they did well from the tradesmen at Christmas (just as they accepted many a glass of sherry while placing orders in the village shops at other times), and clearly there was great scope for dishonesty from a few.

The seniors, particularly the housekeeper, could hire and fire. They had their own servant helpers and they did extremely well out of tips from guests and from perks. Cooks took left-overs, particularly fats, which they sold to cookshops. Butlers sold corks and candle ends (many thousands in a year) and the housekeeper pocketed fees from tourists when they showed them round. Mrs Hulme, housekeeper at Warwick Castle in the early 19th century, accumulated £30,000 in wages and gratuities.

BELOW:
The kitchen and scullery were usually near a staircase leading up to the dining room area. At least one servant was on hand for every three or four members of the family and their guests.

ABOVE AND BELOW:
Liveries could be very elaborate, and footmen and coachmen might be issued with several sets for different occasions. On journeys their baggage was very bulky and might include two or three hat boxes.

Increasingly the more important families spent time in London, and lavished huge sums on their great houses, now almost all demolished. Perhaps the best preserved survivor, the Prince of Wales's Marlborough House, gives only a limited idea of their size and glitter. Another example is Hertford House, the home of The Wallace Collection, in Manchester Square. Just before Easter, servants moved from the country to help the skeleton London staffs to spring clean and prepare for the arrival of the family.

ABOVE:
By the 1850s, race meetings at Epsom and Ascot had almost become public holidays for all types and classes.

GLITTERING PARTIES

The season was a continuous round of parties and dinners, with visits to opera and ballet, art exhibitions, race meetings (particularly at Epsom and Ascot, an hour or so from the West End of London), cricket matches (between Eton and Harrow, and

BELOW:
The most important aristocratic town-houses had the scale and grandeur of palaces.

Oxford and Cambridge), and Henley Regatta. Every day there was riding in Rotten Row, and on some nights there were as many as ten balls. However, for many families the most important occasion was the presentation of débutantes to the monarch at Court in early May.

BUSINESS AND GOSSIP

But there was another side to the London season. Servants and their masters had a chance to meet their friends – both had clubs in London (the footmen's was at a pub, the *Running Footman*, just north of Oxford Street) – to discuss business and exchange gossip. Servants had their own favourite theatres, music and dance halls, and on occasions surreptitiously borrowed their master's and mistress's best clothes in which to visit them.

Their masters could attend parliament, visit their bankers and stockbrokers, order new clothes and perhaps a pair of shotguns, or pay a furtive visit to the nightlife of Paris. Wives and daughters could enjoy a glittering array of shops, and call on girlhood friends normally living far away.

The season ended in early August, when the bachelors went off to the grouse moors or to the yachting at Cowes, while family men, with their broad acres to consider, returned to their country estates to oversee the harvest.

ABOVE:
Rotten Row, a fashionable riding track in Hyde Park since the 17th century – a place in which to be seen!

ABOVE:
After a daughter had been presented at Court, it was the mother's duty to introduce her to as many eligible young men (and their families) as possible.

ABOVE:
Traditionally nursemaids found soldiers to escort them and their young charges on walks in the park; they were said to have 'Scarlet Fever' because of the red tunics worn by the soldiers!

At the end of the London season in August there was a seven month period devoted to country business and pleasure. There were local 'seasons' often arranged to coincide with law sessions and stock sales, when local gentry dined, danced and went to plays together in a local centre like Cheltenham, Bath, Lancaster or York. There were shooting parties and meets of the hunt, with music and cards in the evening. And there were 'Weekend Parties' although this term was considered vulgar until the 1920s.

Edward, Prince of Wales was the ruler of this world. He had invented the country house party when he bought Sandringham in the 1860s and he liked to control proceedings precisely, not only there but by hints and requests at the many houses where he himself became a guest.

Punctuality was of the essence and all the clocks were set 30 minutes fast. Guests travelled on special railway coaches to the local station, where a fleet of carriages met them.

ABOVE:
As in other matters, a landowner considered it important to set an example by farming well. During the 19th century, an estate office was frequently set up, with separate access from a yard so that tenant farmers did not need to pass through the house.

His Royal Highness himself allocated rooms, arranged the seating plan at dinner and organized the programme of entertainments. Woe betide anyone not willing to involve themselves – periodic searches were mounted to flush out the shirkers, hiding behind newspapers or cigar smoke in the billiard room. Clothes, too, were royally approved, and fresh outfits appeared three or four times daily. At 10.30 am, whatever the weather, the shooting party met with a team of uniformed beaters. Ladies were discouraged from attending before lunch, but they had to arrive at the marquee, set up nearby, in time to join the men for some food.

After dinner there were parlour games until the Princess of Wales led the ladies off to bed, when the men could settle down to some serious gambling (except on Sundays) which often lasted till 3.00 or 4.00 am. Houseparties ended on Tuesday mornings, when the Visitors' Book was signed and servants were given their gratuities (known as vails). A generous gratuity was a guinea, the amount some working-class households survived on for a week.

LEFT AND BELOW: Autumn and winter hunting took place when there was little to be done on the land. Most areas had a choice of hunt, and railway companies provided facilities for transporting horses and their owners long distances for an extra day's sport. Food and drink in large amounts for all was the order of the day, and a keen huntsman could, with the aid of a railway timetable, hunt on most days of the week over a wide area.

Hunting, shooting and fishing were the traditional leisure activities of a gentleman. Hunting brought together people from all county families, along with their tenant farmers and members of the professions and the Church. Shooting, of course, had precise seasons in the autumn and winter, except for rabbits and pigeons. Women generally did not like the cold and mud associated with it and men thought they caused accidents with their erratic reactions to the noises, but some did show willing and attend to watch. They tended to remain secluded on their home estates, and activities there were more enterprising. Modern tennis, croquet and archery all evolved on the lawns of the big house and could be played by variable numbers of people and were another way for the well off young to meet potential partners. On occasions, weekend parties were focused on cricket matches.

ABOVE:
Lawn tennis emerged in the 1860s and '70s as a game which could be played by both young men and women on the lawn of the country house. Walking and cycling (once shorter skirts and bloomers began to be tolerated, and after the crossbar had been phased out in the early 1890s) were preferable for ladies in winter.

ABOVE:
By the end of Victoria's reign, country house parties were so well established that entire wings were built to accommodate guests and their servants.

The railway, and much improved road travel from 1880 onwards, meant that the old holiday traditions of the wealthy – summer weeks or months at Brighton or Bath, or up to a year on the Grand Tour of Europe – made way for shorter, more active breaks. Travel for its own sake became a popular form of holiday – cruising on private yachts in the Mediterranean, for instance, or motor car tours, at the very end of the 19th century. The Swiss Alpine flowers were classified and painted, or the mountains climbed, even by ladies. It was at this time that Britons brought the ski to Switzerland from Norway, and introduced the French Riviera to the world of fashion. German and Austrian spa towns became popular for quick 'cures'. They were grander and cheaper than most British watering places, and provided a change of scene. The Prince of Wales set the fashion with annual visits.

WORK OVERSEAS

For many gentlemen the British Empire was of significance as a place for work and trade, often combined with leisure. Representatives of company boards and government departments visited developments in the Dominions to inspect and advise, and journeys were often broken to visit friends and relatives and to sightsee. By the 1870s, when the Suez Canal shortened journeys to India and the Far East, passenger ships were becoming not just safe and fast, but comfortable and even luxurious. Few people as yet looked on a sea cruise as a holiday in itself, but it became possible and fashionable for younger gentlemen to return to Europe from India by way of the railways across the USA or Canada, viewing the size, grandeur and economic potential of the New World.

In all these activities, servants went along too, and the youthful strength and flair of the best valets made them valuable companions.

ABOVE:
By the end of the 19th century passenger ships were safe and fast, and became increasingly luxurious as the popularity and necessity of sea travel grew. Valets would often accompany their masters on trips overseas.

BELOW:
On any journey, every member of the entourage, family or servant, needed a great deal of luggage.

ABOVE:
The village girls in most laundries had high complexions because of the heat. Perhaps it made them more attractive to the coachmen and other young men. Of course there were always illicit love affairs among servants but, if they came to the master's attention, instant dismissal was the rule.

Even in the later decades of the 19th century large houses still employed a range of craftsmen. The days were gone when wool from the estate's sheep was turned into cloth and then immediately made into clothes, but there were still carpenters, upholsterers, wheelwrights, butchers and saddlers, and later chauffeurs, gasmen and electricians. The largest group of all consisted of foresters, gamekeepers and gardeners. Sometimes the head gardener had an international reputation for some plant discovery and, like Joseph Paxton at Chatsworth, was held in awe, and paid at the very highest rate for servants. Much activity in the big house went on out of sight, in attics and basements and in service wings screened by trees. The laundry was usually closest to the house, and often staffed by young women from the village. Hot and humid, it was not a popular workplace and perhaps for this reason machinery was introduced there early on, certainly by the 1850s in a few houses. The stables and coach house were often close by. Coachmen and grooms traditionally slept there, to be handy for last minute orders from the family. And in their liveries they cut a dash that was irresistible to the laundrymaids. Most mistresses tried to segregate the house servants, but the job was twice as difficult outside! Attempts were sometimes made not only to make physical contact impossible, but even to prevent looks passing between them, with high walls and screens and separate entrances.

ABOVE:
The estate carpenter frequently made toys for the children in the nursery and occasional pieces of furniture for the house, as well as carrying out repairs.

LEFT:
Most produce came from the estate, even tropical fruit, and an immaculate garden full of exotic plants and furniture was considered a mark of the family's prestige and civilization.

As early as the beginning of the 18th century, those keen on innovation were installing cold water pipes and taps to bathrooms, and then hot water and, finally, towards the end of the century, steam heating. By about 1800, when Bramah's flushing water closet became available, small gasworks could supply domestic lighting and horse driven pumps could fill water tanks in the roof spaces of the big houses. By the 1880s small electricity generators provided a new standard of lighting, though in most big houses these were only introduced gradually. A servant bringing a can of hot water or a tea-tray, and taking away a chamber-pot, was cheaper than installing tanks and pipes, and if things went wrong the remedy was much simpler – instant replacement of the servant!

OTHER OPPORTUNITIES

The most common reasons for a servant to change employment were ambition or a desire to marry. Only very rarely were servants allowed to be married during Victoria's reign, and servants' children were completely banned in the big house. Couples might open a seaside boarding house, shop or inn, and it was not unknown for an ex-master to set them up in business. Young men, with the skills and manners they had acquired, could find posts as shop assistants, and many went into the army. Similarly, young women could find work in the retail trade or in dressmaking, though many became prostitutes.

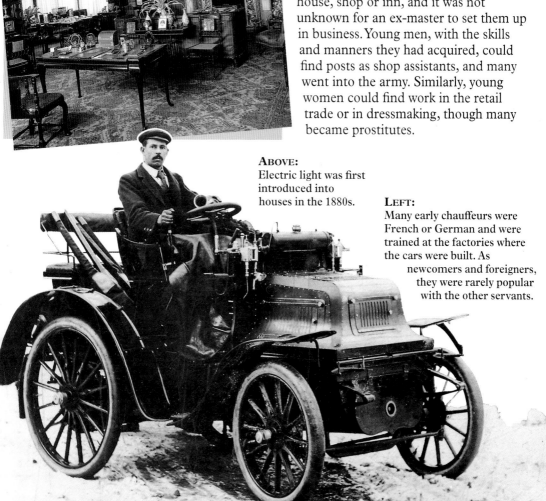

ABOVE:
Electric light was first introduced into houses in the 1880s.

LEFT:
Many early chauffeurs were French or German and were trained at the factories where the cars were built. As newcomers and foreigners, they were rarely popular with the other servants.

ABOVE:
Until the 1880s servants had no proper time off and celebrations were few. However by 1900 many had two half-days per month, as well as time off at Christmas and for household events such as family weddings or coming of age celebrations.

BELOW:
Christmas Day was normally kept for the family's children, with a quieter household routine so that the servants had less work to do. By about 1900 they could look forward to the staff ball, often held on Twelfth Night, and other dances were sometimes held during the year by a few enlightened employers.

Towards the close of the 19th century, staff dances were introduced by some enlightened owners, often held near Christmas, the most important holiday of the year. By the 1850s the Duke of Portland was giving his underground ballroom over to the traditional servants' party, hiring a London band and 50 waiters so that none of his servants had to work.

There was always plenty to eat and drink, and the dancing opened with the master leading the housekeeper onto the floor, followed by the steward with the mistress. At midnight the family melted away, leaving the servants to another three or four hours of carefree enjoyment.

QUIET ENJOYMENT

Presents were often rather dull but generous. At Woburn, footmen received a monogrammed envelope containing a five pound note (perhaps two months' salary) and maids often found a dress length inside their parcel, again worth several weeks' pay. But the same presents tended to be given year after year.

For the family of the house, Christmas Day was not the most important day of the holiday; that was likely to be Twelfth Night. Christmas merrymaking was usually kept to a minimum to give the servants more leisure, and attention focused on the nursery. Both Christmas cards and crackers were British inventions of the Victorian age, while the Christmas tree and Father Christmas were borrowed from the Continent. All of these cropped up in the Christmas of the children of the house, along with carols and games. 'Snapdragon', where nuts and sweets had to be snatched from a bowl of hot brandy, was always particularly popular.